The Truth About Our Existence

By Green Fig

Art & Design By

CHY Illustration & Design

Publisher: Green Fig
Pennsylvania, USA
www.gogreenfig.com
info@gogreenfig.com

Green Fig

Our Journey in life - Second edition
ISBN: 978-1953836441

> Every person is on a journey, and with every step, they are either freeing their soul or destroying it.

CONTENTS

Introduction 5
Chapter 1   God, Our Creator 6
Chapter 2   Before We Came to Be 10
Chapter 3   The Oath 14
Chapter 4   At Conception 16
Chapter 5   At Birth 18
Chapter 6   Accountability 20
Chapter 7   Destiny 22
Chapter 8   Happiness & Money 24
Chapter 9   The Role Models 28
Chapter 10   Jesus, the son of Mary 30
Chapter 11   Death 34
Chapter 12   Paradise & Hell 36
Chapter 13   The Journey of a Happy Soul 38
Conclusion   What's in Your Heart? 40

Introduction

What is the purpose of our existence on earth? Where did we come from and where are we going to? Do you know what will happen to you after you die? These are questions that many of us at some point in our life thought about. We cannot attain fulfillment in our journey without knowing the ultimate truth in this life.

As Muslims entrusted with true knowledge, adherents to the one true religion, the religion of all the prophets, we have the answer to all these questions and more, and we use this knowledge to pursue happiness in this life and afterwards. Since our knowledge is derived from the teachings of the prophets, who received revelation from God, it is free from misguidance and error.

The primary purpose of humankind is to worship the Lord rightfully. This knowledge translates into a way of life, actions and choices directed toward fulfilling that purpose. The guidance for humanity is conveyed by the prophets who are chosen by God and sent to show us the path that leads to true success in this life and in the Hereafter.

This book is dedicated to each one seeking the true path in the journey of life. May yours be enlightened!

God, Our Creator

Can there be a building without a builder? Can there be a writing without a writer? Of course not. How about this whole universe with all its complexities and order? Surely, it must have a creator! A Creator who gave each creation its particular attributes. Look no further than yourself, and you can see how the fascinating composition of the human body is sufficient proof for a sound mind that there is a Creator. And beyond the visible structure of flesh and bone, the human being is composed of both body and soul. Such a union cannot be accidental; it requires a Creator who willed that such union take place.

Now think about your inner self. Your emotions shift. Your thoughts waver. Your determination breaks. Such constant change is a sign that we are dependent and created. And what is created cannot exist without a Creator.

We exist; therefore, we must have one who brought us into existence. It is impossible that a person created himself because this entails that this person existed before himself to be able to create himself. Whatever has a beginning needs one who brought it into being.

It is also impossible for nature to be the creator because nature does not have a will. Nature itself has a beginning and needs a creator that created it along with the rest of the universe. The universe exists because God willed for it to exist. Hence, our

Chapter 1

existence and that of the whole universe is a proof of God's existence.

There is no knowledge more important in your life than knowing the One who created you. God existed before all creation. He is eternal, without beginning, while everything else has a beginning. He is the Creator, and all else is created. He alone brings all things from nonexistence into existence.

Change surrounds us. We see it in ourselves, in our bodies, in our thoughts, in our circumstances, and in the world we live in. We see it in growth and decline, beginning and ending, movement and stillness. Our bodies age with time. Our desires appear and disappear. Our emotions rise and fall; we may love and then grow angry, feel hopeful and then discouraged, sometimes within the span of a single conversation. Our resolve weakens and strengthens. What we feel strongly in one moment may fade in the next; what we decide today we may undo tomorrow. Change is indeed a mark of creation. But God is not subject to change. Unlike creation, He is not affected by time or transformation. What changes move from one state to another. This implies need, deficiency, or development. But the Creator is not in need, and His perfection does not increase or diminish; it is complete and does not evolve.

True understanding begins with recognizing that God is not like anything. He is not an entity that has dimensions, nor is He composed of parts like the bodies that make up the universe. He is not like humans or angels, nor like light or souls.

God does not need anything; need belongs to the creation, not the Creator. After creating the universe, He did not become dependent on it. He does not need humans or angels, nor the earth or the heavens, nor even time or place. Time and place pertain only to what is created. Time passes over creation, for whatever has a beginning is subject to it. And it is creation that needs place. God is not encompassed by time nor confined by space. Time and place came into existence with creation. God existed before time and place, before light and darkness, before angels and humans, before earth and heaven.

Knowledge of God is not attained through imagination or illusion. We cannot picture Him, for whatever we imagine belongs to creation—and God is not a creation nor similar to any creation. We know God but we cannot have the knowledge of His reality. He exists now as He has always existed, without beginning and without end.

Before We Came to Be

The first creation that God created was water. From that original water, God created everything else. After the water, the Throne (Al-'Arsh) was created, followed by the Upper Pen, followed by the Guarded Tablet, followed by the souls.

God commanded the original water into existence, and it came into being. It began to exist after being non-existent—without an origin. From this original water God created everything else, alive or innate either directly from water or with other creations in between. The first thing God created from water was the ceiling of Paradise, known as the Throne (Al-'Arsh) which is a platform with pillars and the largest creation in size. The Throne is like a Kaabah to the numerous angels that surround it. The Throne was created above the water. God made time, place, and directions enter into existence along with the creation of the original water and the Throne. The next thing that God created from water is the Upper Pen. It is similar to light in form and as tall as the distance between the earth and the first sky. After this Pen, God created the Guarded Tablet, in the form of one giant pearl, the surface of which is the distance of 500 years, surrounded on both sides with rubies. The Pen was

Chapter 2

ordered to write on the Guarded Tablet all that will occur until the Day of Judgment. The Pen wrote as it was commanded without anyone holding it. After 50,000 years, God created the heavens, the earth, and all that is between them in six days, each equivalent to a thousand of our years. On Sunday and Monday, God created the earth. On Tuesday and Wednesday, God created the seven heavens. On Thursday and Friday, God created the mountains, rivers, trees, valleys and the other landmarks of the earth. Close to the beginning of Friday, God created all the angels from light. On that day, God created Satan, who one of the jinn and the head of the devils, from smokeless fire. Toward the end of Friday, the first man, Adam, was created. Adam was the last kind of the creations—humankind. Humans live only on this earth and nowhere else. No humans live on the other six earths that exist below this earth, but jinn and animals do.

Adam was created from soil. An angel was commanded to gather from every type of soil—the red, the white, the black, and shades in between; the smooth and the rough; the good and the bad. This soil was taken to Paradise and was mixed and kneaded with water from underneath the Throne. The shape of Adam was molded from this clay. Consequently, the offspring of Adam differ in color and character the same way the soils that

Adam was created from differ. After this clay dried and hardened, God turned it into flesh, bones, and blood. When the soul was blown into this body, Adam became alive. Adam sneezed and the first thing he uttered was, "I praise the Lord of the worlds" in Arabic. Adam was beautiful, sixty cubits tall, and spoke eloquently. God created Eve from the left shortest rib of Adam and made her his wife. Lady Eve was also created as an adult commensurate in height to that of our master Adam. Adam and Eve loved each other and lived happily in Paradise. After 130 years, Adam descended with Eve to the earth. With them descended all the fruits which changed when planted on earth.

Adam became a prophet on earth and received the revelation through Angel Gabriel. He lived till he saw forty thousands of his offspring. God gave Adam the knowledge of all languages though most of his conversation with his children was in Syriac. God also gave him the knowledge of obtaining a living; Adam knew how to plant wheat, a crop that descended from Paradise too, how to harvest it, and how to make it into bread. Adam knew how to extract iron, make fire, and how to coin money from gold and silver. Our master Adam taught his children all these skills and other beneficial types of knowledge. Most importantly, Adam taught his children about Islam and how to worship God.

Chapter 3

The Oath

Souls are among the earliest creations. Every human soul—of those who lived before us, those alive now, and those yet to be born—existed during the time of Prophet Adam. For a period, they were contained within his back. Then God brought forth the souls of all Adam's offspring and gathered them in a valley near Mecca, in the region of 'Arafat. He gave them a human form, as small as red ants. He instilled within them knowledge, and they recognized Him as their Creator.

There, they professed God's Lordship. An angel conveyed to them the divine question: "Am I not your Lord?" They said, "Yes, we testify." Every soul affirmed that it had no Lord except Him. Every soul acknowledged its Creator and testified to His Oneness—including yours. This moment is known as the Day of Alastu—from the Arabic Alastu, meaning "Am I not?"

Later, when the soul enters the body in the mother's womb, it forgets that gathering and the covenant it made. Yet something remains. Though we are born knowing nothing, we come into this world prepared to recognize our Creator and ready to return to the knowledge our souls once possessed. When the message of faith reaches the heart, it awakens something that was already affirmed long ago.

Because of what happened that day sometimes we meet somebody that we did not know before and we feel an immediate connection like we have known that person for a long time. This is because of the souls' meeting and their homogeneity and agreement on that ancient day.

Chapter 4

At Conception

The beginning of human formation occurs at conception. The Qur'an describes the human being as created from a gushing fluid emerging from between the backbone and the ribs. This refers to the reproductive fluid of the male originating from the loins, and that of the female originating from the region of the chest. In Islamic terminology, this fluid is known as maniyy—the reproductive fluid of both male and female. When these fluids are brought together within the woman's body, and if God wills, their union results in conception. At this earliest stage, what exists is only the physical beginning of human formation. The soul has not yet been breathed into it.

Human development in the womb takes place in stages. For the first forty days, the human being begins as a tiny drop—the combined reproductive fluid of the male and female. Then for another forty days, it becomes a clinging form. Then for another forty days, it develops into a small, formed lump. After this, an angel is sent, and the soul is breathed into it, 120 days after conception.

The soul was created before the body. At the appointed time in the womb, the angel is commanded to bring the soul destined for that body and unite it with the fetus. At this point the fetus becomes alive and a new stage of existence begins.

The reality of the soul is known only to God. Our knowledge of the soul is very limited. We know that it is an impalpable body, which, as long as it is inside the body of a human, angel, jinn or an animal, this body is alive. Death occurs when the soul completely separates from the body. Not all souls are alike. Some are honored, while others are not.

The soul, like everything else in this universe, has a beginning. God brought it from nonexistence into existence. The soul is not part of God. God creates by His will and power; nothing is part of Him.

Actually, each one of us passes through two deaths and two lives. We were first lifeless—a tiny drop in the womb, without a soul. God then gave us life. Later, at the end of our earthly lives, He causes us to die. And on the Day of Resurrection, He brings us back to life once more.

We were lifeless before the soul was given to us. We live, we die, and we will live again!

Chapter 5

At Birth

None of us chose to enter into existence. This proves that we did not create ourselves nor did our parents create us for a human cannot create another human. A body cannot bring another body into existence. That which creates bodies cannot itself be a body—neither a physical body like ours nor a subtle created being like the soul.

We are all born in accordance with the oath that was taken from the souls on that ancient day, ready to recognize and accept the truth of Islam when it is presented to us, returning to the state of belief we once affirmed. However, when we are born, the soul does not remember that day because so much time has lapsed since.

Prophet Adam was the first human. He was created without a mother or father, and he was created as an adult, with knowledge and understanding instilled in him. We, however, are born as infants without understanding. By the time a child reaches the age of discernment, the child begins to understand what parents and others say and usually accepts what is taught.

We are born crying. A metaphor that the baby has left the safety of the womb and entered into the world, a world of hardships, happiness mixed with sorrow, pleasure and pain, and calamities!

Chapter 6

Accountability

Everything that happens in this universe is by the decree of God. Nothing, whether entities or deeds, comes into existence except by God's will, knowledge, and power. This includes our voluntary and involuntary actions.

God endowed humans with a will that allows us to make choices. We are not like a feather that is swayed right and left depending on which way the wind blows. Everyone experiences a clear distinction between voluntary and involuntary deeds, as exemplified by the difference between a sick person's unintentional tremors causing them to knock over a cup of coffee, and someone intentionally hitting the cup and spilling the coffee.

What is special about the voluntary actions is that they are the deeds related to acquisition, for which we are either rewarded or punished in the Hereafter. For every soul, what it acquired is either for or against its benefit. Therefore, the human being is not compelled, nor is he forced to act, because compulsion negates accountability. God creates our actions, and we are responsible and accountable for the choices we make.

Chapter 7

Destiny

God is the Creator of everything. He has willed the existence of all creation, and among it are both good and evil. All of them occur by His eternal destining, knowledge, and power. Nothing occurs except by His will, and none can prevent the fulfillment of what He wills.

Yet human beings act and are accountable for their actions. As the Early Muslim scholar Abu Hanifah (699-767) states in his book *Al-Fiqh Al-Akbar*:

"God brought forth the offspring of Adam from his back, in forms as small as tiny red ants, and endowed them with intellect. He commanded them to believe and forbade them from disbelief. They affirmed His Lordship and that affirmation was faith from them. Therefore, they are born with the innate readiness to accept the belief in one God when presented to them. Whoever disbelieves thereafter has changed that state, while whoever believes and affirms remains firm upon it. God did not compel any of His creation to disbelieve or to believe, nor did He create them as believers or disbelievers; rather, He created them as persons. Belief and disbelief are the acts of the slaves. God eternally knows each person in whatever state they are in;

if their state changes, neither His Knowledge nor His attributes change. All the actions of the slave, whether motion or rest, are truly acquired by them while God is their Creator, and all occur by His knowledge, will, decree, and ordainment.

All acts of obedience are by His command, love* [meaning His will to grant goodness and reward], acceptance, knowledge, will, decree, and ordainment; and all acts of disobedience are by His knowledge, decree, ordainment, and will—but not by His love, acceptance, or command‡."

*When love (maḥabbah) is attributed to Allah, it does not refer to emotional states as experienced by human beings, but to His will to bestow goodness and reward. His attributes are affirmed as befits His Majesty, without resemblance to creation.

‡Will is an eternal attribute of God. By His will, He determines which possible things come into existence, with their particular qualities and at their appointed times. Nothing occurs outside or in opposition to His will.

God's will is distinct from His command. He may command something without willing that it occur. For example, God commanded Prophet Abraham to sacrifice his son, yet He did not will that the sacrifice take place; instead, a ram was provided in his place. Likewise, God commands human beings to do good and avoid sin, yet not all people obey. Their actions occur by His will—not against it.

Happiness & Money

"Richness is not in having many possessions; true richness is the contentment of the soul." Prophet Muḥammad

Much is said about happiness. Many insist they are chasing it, yet few pause to ask what it truly is. Is it something you possess, or a state you become? Can it be purchased by collecting more things, or by climbing higher in wealth? Too often, people misunderstand happiness. While pursuing what they perceive is "happiness", they are in reality running toward their own exhaustion and ruin. So let's get some principles clarified.

To begin with, more possessions do not guarantee more happiness. We have all heard the saying that money cannot buy happiness, and it can be difficult to accept at times, especially for those who feel they have never had enough. Many only learn this lesson after paying for it with years of restless striving. Yet the wise do not spend their lives chasing riches in the hope that the next acquisition will finally deliver contentment. They understand that wealth is a tool, not a destination. They use what they have to support a good life, rather than sacrificing their peace to gather more.

Yes, certain comforts can contribute to ease and pleasure—a spacious home, a beautiful view, the relief of stability. But these things were never meant to be the purpose of our existence. In fact, much of what brings the sweetest satisfaction is either free

Chapter 8

or inexpensive. Consider how the same meal tastes far more delightful after hunger; it is not always the food that changes, but our awareness and gratitude. We are encouraged to notice what we have so we can truly enjoy it. Even psychologists recommend practices of gratitude, like writing down blessings, to strengthen the sense of wellbeing.

The truth is the person who awakens secure among his people, healthy in body, and with enough provision for the day possesses a treasure so great that it is as if he owns the whole world. Yet many do not recognize their blessings until they disappear—whether health, relationships, safety, or stability.

A wise man once presented a rich ruler with a question: if you were deprived of water and death by thirst was near, what would you pay for a single drink? The ruler replied, "Half of what I own." Then the wise man asked: if that water could not leave your body, what would you pay to be relieved of it? The ruler said, "The other half." The wise man concluded: what sort of kingdom is worth no more than a drink of water and the ability to expel it?

Money is not the same for everyone. While it can be a great blessing, too often it becomes a burden. Many are blinded by envy and consumed by greed. They commit wrongs to obtain wealth, or they spend it in ways that corrupt them, pulling themselves away from goodness. And what is the value of someone who gains the world yet loses his own soul? Reality eventually exposes the truth, though for many it is discovered too late. It is painful to watch people, of every background and every financial status, depart this world and leave behind their wealth, sometimes to those who resent them, when that very wealth could have been used wisely to benefit them before death. A smart person uses every means to better his life and character and invest in what truly matters. This is when true happiness begins.

In this life, there are moments of joy and moments of sorrow.

Feelings pass, whether pleasant or painful. It is an illusion to imagine a life made of uninterrupted happiness. Even if one tasted constant comfort, death would still arrive: the destroyer of pleasures and the separator of loved ones. The undeniable truth is that life is filled with trials, and many hardships are beyond our control. So what should you do? First, adopt a sound mindset and stop sprinting after illusions; you will never catch what was never meant to be held. Then dedicate yourself to goodness, and happiness will accompany you along the way. For a person can remain content even in adversity—through pain, calamity, and difficulty—when guided by clear purpose and committed to what is truly beneficial for oneself and for others.

In the end, it comes down to this: there are two kinds of happiness. There is happiness in this world like a spacious home, a loving spouse, a good neighbor, comfort, and success. Yet this happiness is fleeting. Fragile. Always mixed with worry, loss, and interruption. And then there is happiness in the Hereafter–pure, untouched by disappointment, free from disturbance, and, above all, everlasting. As a wise man once said. "If this world were gold that fades, and the Hereafter mere clay that endures, it would still be wiser to choose what lasts over what perishes. How much more, then, when this world is but fragile clay that passes away, and the Hereafter enduring gold?"

So strive to reach your highest potential. Know why you were created. Invest in the deeds and goals that will still matter when everything else fades. Set your direction toward the place that offers what this world never can. Take the steps, begin the journey, God willing, toward Paradise, where splendid delights abound and joy is complete for both body and soul.

The path to happiness has not been left unclear. The prophets were sent to guide humanity to what brings real wellbeing in this world and lasting enjoyments in the next. The truly successful are those who walk that path.

Chapter 9

The Role Models

God sent thousands of prophets to humans to teach them what will save them in the Hereafter and what will benefit them in this life. As the best of all creation, they were entrusted with revelation and perfected in character. This is why they are our role models. All prophets are men; they are indeed humans, but have merits over other humans. God granted them impeccability. They are protected from blasphemy and from major sins. Among minor sins, they are protected from anything that reflects baseness or compromises their noble character. God sent the prophets to call for Islam, the only true religion and the religion of all the prophets. God is wise. He sent prophets, all attractive in manners and in figure, elements that help in their mission. All prophets are beautiful, eloquent, pure, patient, trustworthy, truthful, courageous and endowed with superb mental capabilities. They all told the people that only God deserves to be worshipped. They warned them about Hellfire and gave the good news of Paradise.

God sent the prophets as a mercy to mankind. The one who follows the prophet is a winner, and the one who refuses their call has only himself to blame. God supported all prophets with miracles—extraordinary signs that confirmed their truthfulness. Those who opposed them were unable to produce anything similar or to refute them. If a person rejects the prophet's call after witnessing such a miracle, or after hearing of it in a manner that leaves no room for denial, that rejection is nothing but arrogance—a refusal to accept what a sound mind sees as clearly proven true. Once such proof becomes clear and the message reaches us, we are left without excuse.

All prophets worshiped One God who does not change. All of them had the same belief. What differed is some of the rules that changed over time because of a wisdom. This rule would carry the best interest at the time it was revealed. For example, Muslims now pray five times a day. At the time of Prophet Adam, Muslims prayed once a day. The last Prophet is Prophet Muḥammad. Therefore, the rules revealed to him are the last ones to be revealed; they won't be cancelled or superseded by any other set of rules. It carries the interest of the people until Judgment Day.

Chapter 10

Jesus, the son of Mary

Before Judgment Day, Jesus, peace be upon him, will appear. Prophet Jesus is still alive. He did not die yet. He lives in the second sky like angels do without food and water. This is so because God is the Creator of food and health. Food does not create health. Lack of nutrition does not create sickness or weakness. Food, or the lack of it, is just a cause whose expected effect occurs only if God wills.

Jesus was not killed or crucified, rather he ascended to the sky. The one who was crucified was one of his younger companions whom the likeness of Jesus was bestowed on during the last meeting Jesus had with twelve of his companions. When the blasphemers arrived, they saw him, thought he was Jesus and crucified him. This companion will be with Jesus in Paradise. Jesus will descend to the earth and rule it for forty years before Judgment Day. The earth at his time will be full of justice and as a sign of this justice even the wolf will stop attacking the sheep. Jesus will kill the one-eyed False Messiah. His breath will reach the non-believers who will die as a result. Though the breath is not a usual cause of death, but God willed for this to be a cause for the demise of all non-believers. Only the believers will remain at that time. Peace, justice and prosperity will prevail at his time to the extent that if someone wants to give a charity he would not find a poor person. Prophet Jesus might get married and later will die like other humans and will be buried by Muslims near the grave of Prophet Muḥammad in Medina.

Prophet Jesus is not God. Prophet Jesus is created by God.

Chapter 10

Prophet Jesus was created from a mother without a father, like Prophet Adam before him who was created without a father or a mother. The mother of Jesus is lady Maryam, the Virgin Mary, the best woman ever. Angel Gabriel came down and gave Maryam the good news of her immaculate conception east of the Aqsa Mosque in Jerusalem. He blew the honored created soul of Jesus and it entered the body of lady Maryam. Maryam had a strong reliance on God. When the signs of pregnancy became apparent, someone asked her, "Tell me, would plants grow without seeds? Would trees grow without rainfall? Would there be a child without a father?" To all of these questions Maryam replied "Yes." Then she said, "Did you not know that God made the plants emerge without seeds on the day that He created them? Did you not know that God created the trees the first time without rain? Did you not know that God created Adam and Eve without a father or a mother?"

When Jesus was forty days old, God made him speak to defend his mother when people questioned how she had this baby. He professed that he is a slave of God and that he will be given prophethood later in life and that peace was upon him the day he was born and that peace will be upon him the day he will die and the day he will be resurrected. After this time, Jesus did not

speak until the age when children usually speak.

Prophet Jesus did not tell people to worship him or his mother. It is not true that Jesus came to save humankind from the sin committed by Adam as an atonement. Our master Adam, who lived for one thousand years, benefited humanity tremendously. Yes, he did commit a sin—eating from the tree he was prohibited to eat from in Paradise—but it was a small sin that did not reflect any baseness or defect in his noble character, and he repented immediately from it and God accepted his repentance. Humanity does not bear the burden of this sin. The repentance from this sin long occurred and no burden of it is reflected on Adam's offspring. Each one of us is born without any sin; it is later on in life that we acquire sins when we commit them. Moreover, if a parent commits a sin, the children do not bear the responsibility of that sin. Each one is responsible for one's own deeds!

When Jesus descends to the earth, he will break the cross and kill the swine, restoring the worship of God as it was originally revealed. He will rule according to the revelation given to the final prophet, Muḥammad, peace be upon him and upon all the prophets.

Chapter 11

Death

"The smart one is the one who calls himself to account and does noble deeds that benefit him after his death."
Prophet Muḥammad

Death is the sure thing that is going to happen to everyone. We are all going to die, whether rich or poor, sick or healthy, happy or miserable. But the question is: in what state will we die? Because death is just a door. What's behind this door?

It is ironic that many in this life seek immortality, even some might ask for their body to be frozen after death, in case, illusioned, they might be revived again in this life. Actually, immortality is the fate of every one of us—but not in this world. So are you ready? Do you think about death? If you don't, you should. Remembering death softens the heart. It is not a thought to shy away from, rather it is something that you need to strive to always think of because it will help you to be a better person and to focus on what is beneficial for you. Even in the worldly matters, realizing that one's time on this earth is limited brings both clarity and urgency to one's pursuits. Steve Jobs, Apple co-founder who faced a cancer diagnosis during his life, said in a commencement address at Stanford University in 2005, "Remembering that I'll be dead soon is the most important tool I've ever encountered to help me make the big choices in life."

But the true urgency of death lies not in the temporary, but in what follows it. The wise person uses this awareness to direct their life toward what will hold significance on the deathbed, when the Angel of Death comes to take the soul, rather than investing time and energy in what will not matter then, or worse, in what may become a source of regret. Instead, such a person recognizes the value of embracing Islam, the true religion and the key to everlasting happiness. When one is confronted with the inevitability of death, all the money and accomplishments in the world offer no benefit unless one has made the right choices in this life for ultimate success in the Hereafter.

Eternity awaits each of us. Though for many, it will unfold in a place they never desired. Yes, we are going towards what we are destined to. We are going to make choices, take and miss opportunities, fail at times and succeed at others… until we finish our journey on earth and cross to the Hereafter. This is a journey the outcome of which is unknown to us. We need provisions to cross safely. We need to work towards our happiness, even if we don't know our final outcome; just as the farmer plants the field, while not knowing if he will be able to finally harvest it or whether a flood, a freeze, a disease, or insects are going to prevent him from harvesting his crop.

Chapter 12

Paradise & Hell

"Who would build a home upon the waves of the ocean?! That is like the worldly life, so don't take it as a permanent place."
Prophet Jesus

In the Hereafter, there is only two homes: Paradise or Hell. There is no place in between. At the end, it is either staying forever in Paradise or staying forever in Hell. Which one would you rather have for you and your beloved ones?!

Paradise is located above the seven skies. It is vast, and much bigger than Hellfire, because the traces of the mercy of God are greater than the traces of His punishment. The least one in Paradise will have as much as all this earth and ten more. The life in Paradise is better than what any human on earth can have. Moreover, it is eternal! It is a place when you enter, you don't leave it or desire to leave it. It is a place where you don't get old, sick, tired, bored or sad. It is a place of everlasting youth—all at the age of 33—and happiness. Those in Paradise will experience the enjoyments in body and soul, but the body will be a new body with no defects. There will be wonderful riches, foods, joy, and peace. People will be married and have pleasant interaction with one another.

If it is not heaven for one, it is Hell! Hell is the everlasting dwelling place for those humans and jinn who rejected the call of the prophets. The suffering will be in body and soul. Some, who were followers of the true religion, Islam, will suffer in Hell for some time, because they had sinned, did not repent of their sins during their lifetime, and God did not forgive them. As believers, they will not remain in Hell forever, but will be taken out after a time decreed by God. Then they will enter Paradise and dwell there forever and receive no further punishment. As for the torture of the non-believers in Hell, it is in agreement with their greatest sin, they intended to remain in disbelief as long as they lived, they will be in Hell for as long as they live; and in the Hereafter, since there is no death, this means they will remain in Hell for ever.

Hell is dark. It burned for 1000 years until it became red, then it burned for another 1000 years until it became white, then it burned for another 1000 years until it became black. It is stronger than the strongest fire on earth by seventy times. May God protect us from Hellfire.

If God tortures the sinner, it is by His justice without any injustice; and if He gives reward to the obedient, it is from His generosity with no obligation upon Him, because injustice is only conceived to occur from someone who has a commander and a prohibitor. God has no commander and no prohibitor, so He does as He wills in His dominion, because He is the Creator and the true owner of everything.

Chapter 13

The Journey of a Happy Soul

After the Angel of Death gives the pious person the good news of his successful ending, he takes his soul and hands it to the angels of mercy, who place it in a cloth and ascend with it to the skies. A very pleasant fragrance emanates from the soul. As the angels ascend, they encounter other groups of angels between the earth and the sky, who smell the fragrance and ask, "Who is this good soul?" The angels of mercy answer, "So and so, the son of so and so", saying his name with respect.

As they ascend, the door of each heaven would be opened for them, and they would be greeted by the head of the angels of each heaven, who accompany them until they reach the next heaven. When the soul reaches the seventh heaven, its name would be written in the book of winners. Then, the angels are ordered to return the soul to the earth, and a door from his grave to Paradise will be opened. Before the body is buried, the soul hovers above it, saying, "Make haste! Make Haste!" longing for the enjoyments awaiting it in the grave.

Once the body is buried, the soul joins it in the grave, and stays there until the body decays if it is among those that decay. Then the soul ascends to Paradise and resides there in a shape of a green bird, eating from its fruits and enjoying its gentle breeze. The soul stays there, in enjoyment, until the Day of Judgment, when it returns to earth and joins the resurrected body. After that, the body and soul enter Paradise, assuming their dedicated place in the everlasting abode of happiness.

May God make us among those with happy souls!

Conclusion

What's in Your Heart?

Do you have in your heart what it takes to be saved?

When you use your mind soundly, you know it is impossible for this universe to exist without a Creator. If you see a wounded person, you ask, "Who did this to you?" You do not accept a wound without someone that caused it. So what then of this vast universe and all its complexities? The universe itself bears witness to the existence of its Creator who is unlike anything in creation. After that, we have no excuse. If you are a Muslim, a believer, a follower of the only true religion, Islam, the religion that is supported by the sound mind, remain steadfast in it. Protect your religion more than you protect your most precious possessions. If you are not a Muslim, embrace Islam now. It is easy. By having the correct belief in God and His prophets in your heart and uttering the testification of faith: "I testify that there is no god except God, Allāh, and I testify that Muḥammad, مُحَمَّد Abul-Qasim*, is the messenger of God", you become a Muslim. No need for witnesses or any other ritual to become a Muslim. Take the step that guarantees you everlasting enjoyment. Strive to have a happy ending to your journey in life!

---

* The eldest son of our Prophet was called Al-Qasim. That's why our prophet was also known by "Abul- Qasim" which means the father of Al-Qasim. If a non-Muslim wants to embrace Islam and doesn't know how to pronounce the name Muḥammad correctly because they cannot pronounce the Arabic letter ح, then this person can say instead Abul-Qasim which is easier for many non-Arabs to say. This is worth detailing because if someone utters the testification of faith by pronouncing the name of the Prophet as "Muhammad" (with the sound h after Mu) it would not be valid because our Prophet is not called Muhammad. Please note the sound sim in "Al-Qasim" is pronounced like sim as in "SIM card".

CHY Illustration & Design

Since its inception in 2015, Green Fig got its innovative and unique designs by Chadi Mahdi. Chadi is a professional graphic designer whom together with his daughter Yara, joined forces to establish CHY Illustration & Design. CHY contributes to the majority of Green Fig books and other educational material. CHY ensures that every single drawing is uniquely original and reflective of the essence of the book in scope. The work that CHY does for Green Fig transcends the artistic and aesthetic aspects; in addition to presenting the material in an inviting and fine manner conducive to a clearer thinking, the book design and layout are essential components in making the concept in place more graspable and retainable by the reader.

Follow CHY on instagram at **chy_illustrations** or e-mail them at **illustrationschy@gmail.com**

Green fig is a publishing house specializing in books for children and teens that combine educational depth with cultural and faith-based values, while supporting parents and teachers with impactful educational tools. Green Fig resources serve as a means to nurture children with values that will promote their growth into responsible good-loving individuals.

Though most of our books target the youth, we do also provide selected titles for adults since the happiness and healthy development of a child flourish in an environment surrounded by family members with a sound character and aspirations.

Our books are enjoyed by children and adults alike! They immerse the reader in a positive learning experience by using modalities that engage the mind, heart, and eyes. They encourage the reader to ponder about the world around by looking at it with heightened senses and reflective thinking.

Green Fig takes pride of its special contribution to bring to the modern reader, especially the young ones, the concepts present in the classical authentic texts of the beautiful and moderate religion of Islam in a clear language and format they understand and love. Like a fresh exhilarating breeze, Green Fig smartly designed and conceptualized books intertwined with a rich content, take the reader into a journey where the desired aim is to get closer and closer to "living happily ever after"!

www.gogreenfig.com
info@gogreenfig.com

www.ingramcontent.com/pod-product-compliance
Lightning Source LLC
Chambersburg PA
CBHW041807040426
42449CB00001B/2